Get REAL!

...who you are and why you do those things

A Personality Development Handbook for Teens

by Robert A. Rohm, Ph.D.

Personality
INSIGHTS
Empowering People to Improve

PERSONALITY INSIGHTS, INC.
POST OFFICE BOX 28592
ATLANTA, GA 30358-0592
PHONE : 770.509.7113
FAX: 770.509.1484
www.personalityinsights.com

The
Style
Analysis

GETTING STARTED

> **NOTE:** DO NOT START READING THIS BOOK UNTIL YOU HAVE COMPLETED YOUR OWN STYLE ANALYSIS! You will find it included separately inside this book. Simply follow the directions printed at the top of the white sheet. When finished, follow the instructions at the top of the yellow sheet (the second page of the Style Analysis). When you have finished, return to this page and we'll discover what it all means...!

How to Score Your Graphs...

FIRST: To begin using this page, transfer your **MOST** and **LEAST** responses from your yellow answer sheet to the **MOST** and **LEAST** *scoreboxes* below.

SECOND: In *GRAPH I* below, in the "**D**" column, **circle the number** that corresponds to the number of **D**'s in the **MOST** *scorebox* above it. **Repeat for the *I*, *S*, and *C*.** *(Note: If your exact number does not appear in the graph, circle the next lower number.)* **Do not use your Neutral ("N") number.**

THIRD: In GRAPH II below, in the "**D**" column, **circle the number** that corresponds to the number of **D**'s in the **LEAST** scorebox above it. **Repeat for the *I*, *S*, and *C*.** *(Note: If your exact number does not appear in the graph, circle the next lower number.)* **Again, do not use or worry about your "N's."**

FOURTH: In each graph, connect the circles with a straight line, as shown in the sample graph *(right)*.

PERSONALITY STYLE	D	I	S	C
HIGH	20 16 15	17 10	19 12	15 9
	14 13	9 8 7	11 10	8 7
FAIRLY HIGH	12 11 10	6	9 8	6
AVERAGE (Slightly Above)	9 8 7	5 4	7 6 5	5 4
MID-LINE	6			
	5 4	3 2	4 3	3
AVERAGE (Slightly Below)	3 2	1	2 1	2 1
FAIRLY LOW	1			
LOW	0	0	0	0

ENTER "GRAPH I " NUMBERS

M O S T	D	I	S	C	N	TOTAL
	6	10	1	1	6	**24**

PERSONALITY STYLE	D	I	S	C
HIGH	20 16 15	17	19 12	15 9
	14 13 12 11 10	9 8 7 6	11 10 9 8	8 7 6
AVERAGE (Slightly Above)	9 8	5 4	7 6 5	5
MID-LINE	6			4
	5 4 3	3 2	4 3	3
AVERAGE (Slightly Below)			2	
	2	1	1	2
FAIRLY LOW	1			1
LOW	0	0	0	0

GRAPH I – ENVIRONMENT

ENTER "GRAPH II" NUMBERS

L E A S T	D	I	S	C	N	TOTAL
	3	0	9	10	3	**24**

PERSONALITY STYLE	D	I	S	C
HIGH	0	0	0 1	0 1
	1	1	2	2
FAIRLY HIGH	2	2	3	3
AVERAGE (Slightly Above)	3	3	4	4
	4		5	5
	5	4	6	6
MID-LINE	6	5		7
AVERAGE (Slightly Below)	7 8	6	7 8	8
	9 10 11 12	7 8	10	9 10
FAIRLY LOW	13	9	11	11
LOW	14 15 16 21	10 11 19	12 13 19	12 13 16

GRAPH II – BASIC STYLE

5

Introducing... the Real You!

Now that you have completed your own Style Analysis, this workbook will make great sense to you! Without charting your own personal graphs, everything you read here would be trivia — interesting, but not personally meaningful for you.

See the title on the next page? It says this is not a work book but a *fun* book. And that's the truth! You're going to enjoy meeting yourself in these pages. The *first* time you read this information, you will begin to understand who you are — why you do and say and think the things you do. But you will be returning to these pages over and over again throughout your life — because the second, third, fourth... and *hundredth* time you read this information, you will understand yourself and others more and more!

The first section is the "**Fun Book**," which is used in our Personality Insights' teen seminars. (The blanks are filled in at the seminar. If you are working with this book on your own, the "Answer Key" section provides this information.) The "**Fun Book**" deals with your "motor" and your "compass" — in other words, what drives you and which direction it takes you! There is no "time limit" on understanding this information, so don't feel you have to rush through it. It is the basis for everything else you will be reading.

The next section is "*Making It All Fun.*" It explains how to interpret your graphs and score page, and it shows how your own behavior style is a blend of **D**, **I**, **S** and **C** characteristics.

Following the "Answer Key" section, you will find "*Getting Personal,*" which will help you to apply this information in your life. You can also use this knowledge to motivate other people while learning to cooperate with others according to their personality styles.

The last section is "Getting Focused," and it will help you to plan your future using this new understanding of yourself. Setting goals and knowing how to achieve them is going to be a major part to your success. So let's get going! Let's... **Get Real!**

Get
REAL!

The
~~Work~~ *Fun!* Book

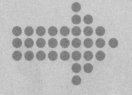

On the following page, you will attempt to find all the numbers, from 1 to 88 in order. You will have one minute — use a timer or a watch to assure accuracy. Circle the number 1... then circle 2... then circle 3, etc., in consecutive order. See how many you can find in 60 seconds.

Ready...? Go!

Don't cheat yourself by looking yet, but the solution is on page 47!

73 9 49 66 78 50
37 53 46 34 62 18
17 5
69 33 1 38 14 74 86
29
41 21 25 10 2 70 22
13 81 77 61 58 54 42
57 85 45 65 6 30 82 26
55 60 80
79 31 32 44
75 63 76
23 47 64 20 40
51 88 68
39 43 3 11 24 4 56
67 71 36
59 87 12
15 35 28 48 16
19 83 72 52
7 27 84 8

Active / Outgoing

your
"motor"

Passive / Reserved

OUTGOING
RESERVED

Task / High-Tech

your
"compass"

People / High-Touch

P
E
T O
A P
S L
K E

Outgoing – Task-Oriented

D
Dominant
Direct
Demanding
Decisive
Determined
Doer

Outgoing – People-Oriented

Inspirational
Influencing
Inducing
Interactive
Impressive
Interested in people
I

OUTGOING • TASK
OUTGOING • PEOPLE
D **I**
C **S**
RESERVED • TASK
RESERVED • PEOPLE

Cautious
Calculating
Competent
Compliant
Contemplative
Careful
C

Steady
Stable
Supportive
Sensitive
Status Quo
Specialist
S

Reserved – Task-Oriented

Reserved – People-Oriented

(Find "fill-in-the-blanks" information for this page on pages 47 and 48.)

Get the Picture...

Most people have predictable patterns of behavior — specific personalities. There are four basic types, also known as temperaments. They blend together to determine your unique personality. To help you understand why you often feel, think and act the way you do, the following is a graphic overview of the Four Temperament Model of Human Behavior.

The four types are like four parts of a pie. Before seeing the four parts as they stand alone, let's look at the pie in two parts. These two types are different from each other. Think of it this way: some people are more *outgoing*, while others are more *reserved*.

Outgoing people are more active and optimistic. Reserved types are more passive and pessimistic. One type is not better than the other. Both types of behavior are important. Reserved types need to learn how to be more **d**ominant and **i**nspirational. Outgoing people need to learn how to be more **s**teady and **c**autious.

Also, there are two other parts of the pie — two other types of personalities. These are also different from each other. Some people are more task-oriented, while others are more people-oriented. Task-oriented types enjoy doing "things" (**d**irecting and **c**orrecting) while people-oriented individuals like to relate with others (**i**nteracting and **s**haring).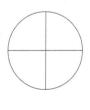

When you look at the four parts of the pie together (as on page 10, opposite), you can visualize the four temperament types. Yet, no one is "purely" one type. **Everyone is a unique blend of these four parts.**

_____
_____
_____
_____
_____
_____
_____
_____
_____
_____
_____
_____

OUTGOING

T
A
S
K

D

*SYMBOL:*_____

*% OF POPULATION:*_____

*EXAMPLES:*_____

*BASIC NEED:*_____

STRENGTHS
STRONG-WILLED
DETERMINED
INDEPENDENT
OPTIMISTIC
PRACTICAL
PRODUCTIVE
DECISIVE
LEADER
CONFIDENT

Remember…
"Weaknesses Are Strengths
— Pushed To An Extreme."

WEAKNESSES
ANGRY
CRUEL
SARCASTIC
DOMINEERING
INCONSIDERATE
PROUD
CRAFTY
SELF-SUFFICIENT
UNEMOTIONAL

UNDER CONTROL ...... OUT OF CONTROL
COURAGEOUS .... RECKLESS
QUICK TO RESPOND .... RUDE
GOAL-ORIENTED .... IMPATIENT
RESULTS-ORIENTED .... "PUSHY"
DELIBERATE .... DICTATORIAL
SELF-CONFIDENT .... CONCEITED
DIRECT .... OFFENSIVE
SELF-RELIANT .... ARROGANT
STRAIGHTFORWARD .... ABRASIVE
COMPETITIVE .... RUTHLESS

(Find "fill-in-the-blanks" information on page 48.)

"D" Types Make Good...

Administrators... school or hospital manager or director
Army Rangers... highly-trained combat soldier
Athletes... sports participant with physical speed, stamina, skill
Blue Collar Workers... industrial worker geared to consistent quality
Boxers... professional skilled offensive/defensive prizefighter
Builders... owner of a building construction business
Business Owners... self-employed, self-directed business operator
Coaches... instructor/manager in charge of a team or game strategy
Construction Workers... craftsman who builds systematically
Developers... person who develops real estate on speculation
Dictators... ruler with absolute power whose word is final
Directors... head of a project or bureau, play or movie
Drill Instructors... military discipline and close-order drill trainer
Entrepreneurs... business organizer who assumes risk for profit
Executives... chief officer managing the affairs of a company
FBI/CIA/DEA Agents... federal investigation and enforcement officer
Fighter Pilots... highly skilled military jet combat flier
Foremen... person in charge of a group of workers in a factory
Gangsters... leader or member of a gang of criminals
Lawyers... advisor in matters of law, representative in lawsuits
Leaders... person directing, commanding, guiding an activity
Marines, Green Berets... special forces, amphibian combat soldier
Military Officers... commander for Army, Navy, Marines, Air Force
Motivators... person who impels or incites the success of others
Navy Seals... underwater espionage and military assault diver
News Anchors... on-air television personality delivering news reports
Pastors... primary leader of a religious congregation
Police Officers... local safety and law enforcement professional
Private Investigator... independent detective
Pro Athletes... employed in highly competitive physical contests
Producers... in charge of financing and coordinating entertainment
Race Car Drivers... high speed competitor and race team leader
State Patrolmen... a law enforcement officer with highway jurisdiction
Supervisors... superintendent or overseer of a work group
Truck Drivers... national or local carrier/deliverer of goods by truck
Students...!

"D" Types Like...

Activity	Hard work
Bigness	Major Productions
Challenge	To be "in charge"
Competition	To fight
Doing Things	Violence

"D" Types...

Can be critical of poorly performed tasks

Complete amazing amounts of work

Need to learn to delegate responsibility

Run roughshod over people

Wrongly believe that approval and encouragement lead to complacency

"D" Types are...

Goal-oriented	Performance conscious
Hard to please	Self-confident
Industrious	Firm

"D" Types Don't Like...

Indecision	Slow people
Lazy people	Taking orders
Slow activities	Talkers who don't produce

"D" Types Want You To Be...

Quick	To the point
Specific	A winner

OUTGOING

**P
E
O
P
L
E**

_____
_____
_____
_____
_____
_____
_____

_____
_____
_____
_____

SYMBOL: _____

% OF POPULATION: _____

EXAMPLES: _____

BASIC NEED: _____

STRENGTHS
FRIENDLY
COMPASSIONATE
CAREFREE
TALKATIVE
OUTGOING
ENTHUSIASTIC
WARM
PERSONABLE
FUN

WEAKNESSES
WEAK-WILLED
UNSTABLE
UNDISCIPLINED
RESTLESS
LOUD
UNDEPENDABLE
EGOCENTRIC
EXAGGERATIVE
FEARFUL

Remember...
"Weaknesses Are Strengths
— Pushed To An Extreme."

UNDER CONTROL	......	OUT OF CONTROL
OPTIMISTIC		UNREALISTIC
PERSUASIVE		MANIPULATIVE
EXCITED		EMOTIONAL
COMMUNICATIVE		GOSSIP
SPONTANEOUS		IMPULSIVE
OUTGOING		UNFOCUSED
FERVENT		EXCITABLE
INVOLVED		DIRECTIONLESS
IMAGINATIVE		DAYDREAMING
WARM / FRIENDLY		PURPOSELESS

(Find "fill-in-the-blanks" information on page 49.)

"I" Types Make Good...

Actors... person who plays roles in television, film, theatre, etc.
Auctioneers... expressive person selling and directing bids at auction
Broadcasters... transmitter of information to a large radio/tv audience
Car Salespersons... explains benefits, induces automobile purchase
Circus Clowns... slapstick comedy entertainers
Coaches... instructor/manager in charge of a team or game strategy
Comedians... comedy entertainer who recites clever monologues
Con Artists... swindler who uses verbal and emotional persuasion
Disk Jockey... radio or party personality who entertains with music
Entertainers... person who amuses with song or dance, etc.
Evangelists... revivalist who holds large meetings in various cities
Flight Attendants... comfort/safety steward on an plane, ship or train
Interior Decorators... designer of living space and functionality
Leaders... person with ability to motivate and direct a group
Masters of Ceremonies... presiding over show, introducing the acts
Peace Corps Volunteers... provider of third-world development help
Politicians... holder of elected governmental office
Preachers... public speaker on religious matters, or sermon-giver
Public Relations Directors... creator of favorable public opinion
Public Speakers... deliverer of speeches, influencing listeners
Reporters... news gatherer/writer for television, radio, newspaper
Salespeople... person employed to sell goods in a retail store
Storytellers... entertainer who narrates tales, anecdotes or stories
Teachers... instructor of lessons, skills, occupations or disciplines
Telemarketers... telephone salesperson, promoter, researcher
Telephone Operators... provider of assistance to telephone callers
Travel Agents... arranger of transportation, lodging for travelers
Variety Artists... performer of magic, juggling, ventriloquism, etc.
Wedding Consultants... planner of formal wedding events
Students...!

"I" Types Like...

Exposure to people

Lots of activity

Short-term projects

To be on the go

Prestige

Selling...while they play
(golf, tennis, etc.)

Making people happy

Making people laugh

"I" Types...

Can be "higher than a kite"
or "lower than a skunk"

Have lots of friends

Need self-discipline

Wrongly believe that
talking and doing
are synonymous

"I" Types are...

Fun to watch

Great starters

Poor finishers

Likeable

Prone to exaggerate

Easily excitable

"I" Types Don't Like...

Being ignored

Being ridiculed

Being isolated

Doing repetitive tasks

"I" Types Want You To Be...

Fun

Responsive

Stimulating

Positive

Upbeat

Enthusiastic

_____

_____

_____

_____

_____

_____

_____

_____

_____

_____

_____

_____

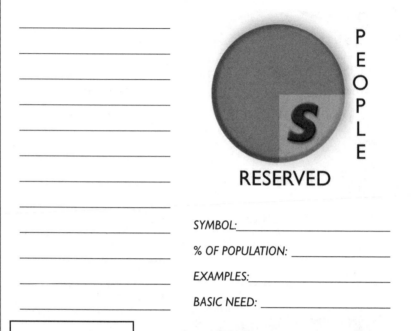

P
E
O
P
L
E

RESERVED

*SYMBOL:*_____

*% OF POPULATION:*_____

*EXAMPLES:*_____

*BASIC NEED:*_____

STRENGTHS
CALM
DEPENDABLE
EASYGOING
TRUSTWORTHY
EFFICIENT
PRACTICAL
CONSERVATIVE
DIPLOMATIC
HUMOROUS

WEAKNESSES
STINGY
FEARFUL
INDECISIVE
SPECTATOR
SELF-PROTECTIVE
UNMOTIVATED
SELFISH
TIMID
SHY

Remember…
"Weaknesses Are Strengths
— Pushed To An Extreme."

UNDER CONTROL	OUT OF CONTROL
RELAXED	LACKING INITIATIVE
RELIABLE	DEPENDENT
COOPERATIVE	A "SUCKER"
STABLE	INDECISIVE
GOOD LISTENER	UNCOMMUNICATIVE
SINGLE-MINDED	INFLEXIBLE
STEADFAST	RESISTS CHANGE
SOFTHEARTED	EASILY MANIPULATED
SYSTEMATIC	SLOW
AMIABLE	RESENTFUL

(Find "fill-in-the-blanks" information on page 49.)

"S" Types Make Good...

Artists... person skilled in fine arts: painting, sculpture, drawing, etc.
Administrative Assistants... support provider for business executives
Chefs... head cook, preparer of gourmet foods in restaurant
Child Care Workers... baby-sitter, nanny, or day care provider
Counselors... advisor on academic, occupational or personal issues
Customer Service Representatives... resolves customer complaints
Department Heads... teacher/professor supervising school faculty
Diplomats... representative/negotiator to foreign country
Electricians... installer/repairer of electrical fittings for home/business
Elementary School Teachers... instructor for younger children
Event Planners... handler of details and hospitality for groups
Flight Attendants... comfort/safety steward on an plane, ship or train
Funeral Directors... mortuary manager, deals with grieving people
Homemakers... a person who manages a household and family
House Painters... craftsman with good technical and people skills
Human Resource Directors... oversees company's personnel needs
Lab Technicians... operator/evaluator of laboratory medical tests
Librarians... supplies/inventories books and educational materials
Managers... handler of business affairs for clients, celebrities
Meeting Planners... coordinator and director of conference details
Nurses... care provider for the sick, in hospital, doctor's office, home
Pharmacists... person licensed to prepare/dispense medicines
Real Estate Agents... representative in buying/selling of property
Researchers... patient gatherer/interpreter of survey data
School Teachers... instructor of lessons, skills, or disciplines
Secretaries... clerical assistant for business operation or office
Social Workers... provider of family health and welfare services
Supervisors... superintendent or overseer of a work group
Teachers... instructor of lessons, skills, occupations or disciplines
Veterinarians... health care for domesticated animals and family pets
Waiters/Waitresses... customer service personnel in restaurants
Writers... a biographer, fiction author, or journalist
Students...!

"S" Types Like...

Peace	Friendly environments
Stabilizing things	To finish the job
To wait	Teamwork

"S" Types...

Are motivated by helping others	Will support you
	Stay with proven methods
Are seldom in a hurry	Are sentimental
Need lots of appreciation	

"S" Types Are...

Easily manipulated	Loyal friends
Reluctant decision makers	Poor starters
The sweetest people in the world	Great finishers

"S" Types Don't Like...

Insensitivity	To be yelled at
Misunderstandings	Sarcasm
Surprises	Being pushed

"S" Wants You To Be...

Kind (not "harsh")	Patient
Pleasant	Understanding

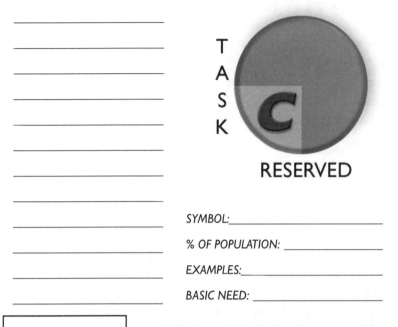

T
A
S
K

C

RESERVED

SYMBOL:_____

% OF POPULATION: _____

EXAMPLES:_____

BASIC NEED: _____

STRENGTHS
GIFTED
ANALYTICAL
SENSITIVE
PERFECTIONIST
AESTHETIC
IDEALISTIC
LOYAL
SELF-SACRIFICING
THOROUGH

WEAKNESSES
SELF-CENTERED
MOODY
CRITICAL
NEGATIVE
RIGID
THEORETICAL
IMPRACTICAL
UNSOCIABLE
REVENGEFUL

Remember...
"Weaknesses Are Strengths
— Pushed To An Extreme."

UNDER CONTROL	...... OUT OF CONTROL
ORDERLY	COMPULSIVE
LOGICAL	CRITICAL
INTENSE	UNSOCIABLE
CURIOUS	"NOSEY"
TEACHABLE	EASILY OFFENDED
CAUTIOUS	FEARFUL
CORRECT	INFLEXIBLE
QUESTIONING	DOUBTFUL
CONSCIENTIOUS	WORRISOME
PRECISE	"PICKY"

(Find "fill-in-the-blanks" information on page 49.)

"C" Types Make Good...

Accountants... person who inspects, keeps, or adjusts account books
Airline Pilots... the operator of a commercial airplane
Architects... person who designs and plans buildings or bridges
Artists... person skilled in fine arts: painting, sculpture, drawing, etc.
Authors... professional writer of books, stories, poems, articles
Bankers... owner or manager of a bank
Bookkeepers... systematic recorder of business transactions
Camera Repairmen... repairer of intricate and complex mechanisms
Carpenters... builder and repairer of wooden buildings, ships, etc.
Chemical Engineers... applies chemistry, physics, math in manufacturing
Choral Conductors... director of vocal music choirs and ensembles
Civil Engineers... infrastructure designer or supervisor
Clerks... office worker who keeps records, types letters, does filing
Composers... creator of complex musical works
Computer Programmers... mathematical/scientific program developer
Consultants... expert called upon for technical advice or opinions
Craftsmen... worker in a skilled trade, such as woodworking
Dentists... person providing care to teeth and surrounding tissues
Draftsmen... drawer of architectural plans for buildings or machinery
Educators... specialist in theories and methods of education
Engineers... specialist in planning/organizing technical operations
Finishing Carpenters... fine work completer of wooden building interiors
Glass Blowers... craftsman or artist who shapes molten glass
Hospital Administrators... long-term planning health services manager
Interior Decorators... designer of living space and functionality
Inventors... deviser of a new method, tool, or contrivance
Lawyers... advisor in matters of law, representative in lawsuits
Librarians... supplies/inventories books and educational materials
Long-Range Planners... detailed business-scheme designer
Machinists... operator of power lathes, punch presses, drills, planers

"C" Types Make Good...(continued)

Mechanical Engineers... production, transmission, use of power/heat
Mechanics... skilled worker using tools to repair cars, trucks, machines
Military Intelligence... gatherer of secret information for military purposes
Musicians... performer, composer or conductor of music
Nurserymen... grower/transplanter of trees and shrubs
Performing Artists... presenter of variety and traditional entertainment
Philosophers... logical analyst of conduct, thought, knowledge, ethics
Photographers... an artist who makes camera pictures
Photojournalists... a news reporter whose pictures help tell the story
Physicians... practitioner of healing arts and medicine
Plasterers... constructor and finisher of walls and ceilings
Playwrights... dramatist who crafts or re-writes theatrical plays
Plumbers... installer/repairer of water or gas pipes, fixtures, drainage
Portrait Photographers... an artist who makes film portraits
Professors... highly-ranked college/university teacher in a specific field
Real Estate Brokers... agent for negotiating, buying and selling property
Sanitation Experts... civil engineer concerned with sewage, water supply
Scholars... specialist in education, especially in the humanities
Scientists... investigator of natural sciences, biology, chemistry, physics
Soloists... performer of music sung exactingly by one person
Specialists... expert concentrating in a particular professional field
Statisticians... expert in manipulation and interpretation of data
Structural Engineers... designer of columns, beams, girders, enforcements
Surgeons... doctor who treats illness by removing diseased tissue
Teachers... instructor of lessons, skills, occupations or disciplines
Theologians... systematic student of religious doctrine and divinity
Theoreticians... specialist in the systems of some art, science, etc.
Tool & Die Maker... makes, maintains, repairs production equipment
Watch Repairmen... repairer/maker of complex timepieces
Students...!

"C"Types Like...

Consistency	Creativity
Detail	Perfection
Confirmation	Orderliness

"C"Types...

Have good imaginations	Have lots of questions
Tend to irritate people	Usually have high I.Q.'s
Tend to be perfectionists	Want directions followed

"C"Types Are...

Impossible to satisfy	Logical
Meticulous	Self-sacrificing
Good thinkers	Talented

"C"Types Don't Like...

Being criticized	Mistakes
Sudden changes	Unnecessary interruptions
Hypocrites	Broken promises

"C"Types Want You To Be...

Accommodating	Accurate
Honest	Careful
Accountable	Analytical

Review of Traits

OUTGOING

Style: Dominant • Determined

Main Features: Good problem solver; risk taker; strong ego; self-starter; goal oriented

Value to Group: Good motivator; good at organizing events; high value on time; results-oriented

Danger Zones: Argumentative; does not like routine; oversteps authority at times; can be pushy

Greatest Fear: Someone taking advantage of them

Style: Inspirational • Influencing

Main Features: Outgoing; talkative; enthusiastic; impulsive; persuasive; optimistic

Value to Group: Good encourager; good sense of humor; peacemaker; creative problem solver

Danger Zones: Inattentive to detail; prefers popularity to doing right; "convenient" listener; disorganized

Greatest Fear: Rejection; loss of social approval

T A S K

P E O P L E

Style: Cautious • Correct

Main Features: Thinks things through; accurate; high standards; careful; systematic; precise

Value to Group: Good organizer; follows directions; even-tempered; clarifies situation well

Danger Zones: Finds fault easily; so focused on detail may miss big picture; too critical

Greatest Fear: Criticism of their work and effort

Style: Supportive • Steady

Main Features: Warm; friendly; understanding; patient; easygoing; good follow-through

Value to Group: Good listener; team player; loyal; reliable; dependable; works well under authority

Danger Zones: Resistant to change; "stuffs it" inside; difficult establishing priorities; sometimes oversensitive

Greatest Fear: Loss of security and stability

RESERVED

This chart shows other comparisons between the basic styles.

Characterizing Question:	**WHAT?**	**WHO?**	**HOW?**	**WHY?**
Descriptive Color:	("Go!") Green	("Flashy") Red	("Serene") Blue	("Cautious") Yellow
Behaves like this Animal:	Doberman	Fluffy Puppy	Cat	Tropical Fish
Ideal Car:	Mercedes Cadillac	Convertible	Van Station Wagon	Toyota Honda
Motivation Motto:	"Go for it!"	"Lighten up!"	"All for one... one for all!"	"If something can go wrong, it will!"
Theme Song:	"I Did It My Way" "Rocky"	"Celebration" "Don't Worry, Be Happy"	"Lean on Me" "I'm Your Puppet"	"The Gambler" "Tell me Why"
Overall Philosophy:	"I want it yesterday!"	"Let the good times roll!"	"Working together, we can do it!"	"Don't show all your cards!"
Interesting Magazine:	Money	People	Us or Parents Magazine Reader's Digest	Consumer Reports
Target Practice Call:	"Ready...Fire... Aim!"	"Ready...Aim... Talk!"	"Ready...Ready... Ready...."	"Ready...Aim... Aim...Aim..."
Motivating Need:	Challenge Dominance	Recognition Interaction	Appreciation Support	Quality Answers Correctness

Get
REAL!

Making
It all
Fun! ~~Work~~

Interpreting Your Score Page...

First of all, remember — *you are you!* You are not a different person at home from who you are at work, or at a party, or at a ball game. Your *behavior* may be *demonstrated differently*, or your *environment* may demand your performance in a role that is not exactly comfortable for you. However, you are still you. It is a false assumption to think in terms of being "two people." It is more accurate to see yourself in two different *behavior styles*: your **Environment** Style and your **Basic** Style — which is what your two graphs on page 5 reflect.

On page 5, *GRAPH I* is your "**Environment**" graph. It reveals how you expect yourself to "perform" — the way you believe you should be at school or work, in order to achieve success. To some degree, your environment influences the way you feel, act and think. The family to which you belong, the events in your childhood, and the culture from which you come — all have had a vital role in creating the person you are today. Psychologists often refer to this as "**nurture.**" Over time, *GRAPH I* tends to be more changeable, especially with changes in your environment, experience, maturity level, or personal inward growth. We should all seek to adapt or adjust our behavior throughout life as different situations or circumstances demand.

NOTE: *GRAPH I* has the word "**MOST**" printed above it, because it comes from all the phrases you selected in the "**MOST**" category. We tend to see ourselves in a role we think we *should* meet to achieve success. (Notice that the plotting point numbers on *GRAPH I* are shown from **HIGH** at the top to **LOW** at the bottom. The more choices you made for each "**D-I-S-C**" category, the higher your plotting point for that trait.)

GRAPH II is your "**Basic Style**" graph. It is your comfort zone, the way you are "wired." It shows how you operate on "automatic pilot," when you are totally at ease. It is the "real you." To a certain degree, your personality is formed by your genetic makeup, inherited from your parents. You are "designed" a certain way from birth, apart from any outside influences, and your unique DNA chain — your "gene graph" — contains characteristics from many generations. These make you the only, unique, special one like you in the world! Psychologists refer to this part of our behavior as "**nature**." This chart/graph tends to remain more constant throughout life.

NOTE: *GRAPH II* has the word "**LEAST**" printed above it. This word "least" does not describe qualities which are less dominant in your personality. The word "least" is used because this graph shows **your selections** taken from the "**LEAST**" category — what you said you are *least* like. In other words, your selections show the kinds of behaviors you tend to avoid. Unlike *GRAPH I*, these **plotting point numbers** chart from **FEWER** at the top (the top of the graph is the "strong" area) to **MORE** at the bottom (the bottom of the graph is the "weaker" area). For *GRAPH II*, look at your plotting points **location** (high or low) rather than your plotting point **numbers**. This view allows you to see your natural or "**Basic Style**" from an additional perspective.

So, GRAPH I shows your "**nurture**," while *GRAPH II* shows your "**nature**." Both graphs will probably look fairly similar. Differences in the two graphs will be explained later in this book.

How many different graphs are there?

Based on available choices among the 24 "**MOST**" phrases, a total of 19,680 *different* graphs could be drawn. And, combined with another 19,680 *different* graphs from the 24 "**LEAST**" phrases, a potential 39,360 *different* **graphs** are possible! (Is it any wonder there are so many differences in the world?)

However complicated this may seem, most of the general population falls into just 16 basic personality styles or behavior blends. Our assessment process of 28 styles (pp. 36–43) will yield an accurate profile for most readers. (A computerized assessment is available from Personality Insights that is capable of producing 368 different graphs and reports for almost 100% of the general population.)

So, each person's graph has a potentially different "*D-I-S-C*" score. The *D-I-S-C* plotting point ranges can be high or low in either graph. As you can see, the magnitude of these numbers makes it impossible to write a complete evaluation for each potential graph. There would be too much unnecessary repetition.

Reading your graphs...

Your two graphs may be very similar, or they may be different — they do not indicate "flaws" in your character, but the "differences" in your personality. To review, the letters represent these traits:

D - Dominant
I - Inspirational
S - Supportive
C - Cautious

If your chart shows that your "**D**" is high, that means you have a lot of **dominance** in your personality style. If your "**D**" is low, that means you are low in dominance. If your "**D**" is close to the mid-line, you are not particularly strong or weak in that quality. This holds true for the "**I**," "**S**," and "**C**" traits, as well.

The "**D-I-S-C**" scores in these two graphs simply show the difference in how you *respond* in your environment, compared to how you *really feel* inside. The more these two graphs are alike, the more comfortable you will probably feel in *what you do* and *who you are.*

For many people, their two graphs will be similar in appearance, although they may have one or two plotting points that seem to differ. Where you find a difference, compare the charting points to see in which areas you are high or low — and whether this occurs in your "**Environment**" or in your "**Basic Style.**"

When you see a very significant difference, it may mean that some environmental factor is clashing strongly with your natural inclinations. (If you were "born to juggle" you will probably not enjoy being a tax accountant.) Often, young people "try on" behavior styles to find out what "fits" and feels comfortable. (More about that on page 44.) A significant difference might also indicate that you are going through some major challenges, and this assessment may provide clues for finding a better balance. Just remember, your behavioral style is not "right" or "wrong" — it is just *you!*

SCORE Analysis Graph Examples

1. A person may score a higher "***D***" in their "**Environment**" graph (***GRAPH I***) than they score in their "**Basic Style**" graph (***GRAPH II***). This indicates that they have *learned* they must be more dominant and direct in their environment, but it is not the way they *really feel* inside.

2. A person could score a low "***I***" in their "**Environment**," but a high "***I***" in their "**Basic Style**." This would mean that in their environment, they have learned they cannot be very inspirational or impulsive — but they would really like to be. That would allow them to be more comfortable.

3. A person might score high in their "***S***" — both in their "**Environment**" and in their "**Basic Style**." This means they enjoy being able to serve and support in their environment, because it is also their "**Basic Style**."

4. A person could score high in their "***C***" in their "**Environment**" but low in their "**Basic Style**." This would mean that in their "**Environment**" they know they must be cautious and correct, but their "**Basic Style**" reveals that is not how they *really feel* inside. To perform successfully, they have found ways to "raise their '***C***'" in their "**Environment**."

Again, there is no "right" or "wrong" personality style — just *different*. The closer your plotting point is to the *top* of either graph, the *more dominant* that trait is in your personality — and the closer your plotting point is to the *bottom* of either graph, the *less dominant* that trait is in your personality. By understanding how these two graphs work together, you can understand your own style more clearly.

Just for fun...

In order to value and appreciate ourselves and each other, we need to understand ways in which we are different. And since there are no "right" and "wrong" personalities, but *differences* in the way we are "wired," you should not feel embarrassed to show your graph to another person. If you both understand the basics of personality styles, you may already have guessed what the other's personality style is, anyhow!

So, when you compare your chart with another person's report, review your plotting points to discover areas of similarity and difference. Some of what you see should help you to better understand and respect each other's gifts and skills.

Often, it is our differences that attract us to each other. Unfortunately, those differences may begin to wear us down after awhile. *Yet, it is in our unique differences that we help and complement one another. We really do need each other!*

One final thought: There are numerous testing instruments, assessments and surveys available today. No one has a "perfect tool" that can *make* you get your life under control. Sometimes, good counseling, right friends, proper rest, exercise and a correct diet will do a lot of good! If you feel you need further help, seek it. This assessment is simply meant to be a useful tool in understanding yourself better, as well as helping you to recognize that other people have behavioral styles that are different from your own.

Blends

As you have read through this material, you have probably found yourself thinking, "I feel a lot like this one personality style, but I also feel like I have some of the other styles in me, too." You do — it should be obvious that *no one is purely a "D," "I," "S,"* or *"C."* No one will fit neatly and nicely into *just one* personality style.

You will always find yourself identifying with some of the behaviors and preferences of other personality types. For survival, you have learned to accommodate your own style to a variety of different situations.

However, this experience of adjusting yourself to your situation has probably made it difficult for you to identify and separate your *acquired* or environmental traits from your *natural* or genetic traits. So, how can you identify your most dominant personality style? You can begin by seeking to understand what *drives* you — that is, what your *passion* is, rather than just what you are doing each day to get by.

At times, circumstances force you to use a particular style with which you are very uncomfortable. But adapting yourself to these circumstances will also cause you to grow in new areas. Remember, you are not completely lacking in personality skills in any of your own, less dominant *"D," "I," "S,"* or *"C"* areas!

The chart on the following page shows how each style is "connected" to the styles adjacent to it. This indicates that your own particular style "bleeds over" into, or borrows from, other personality types. "Borrowing" from your other, less dominant traits is part of fitting in and working with others.

You may have noted from your own experience that the style which is *diagonally opposite* your primary style (*"D"* and *"S"* are opposites, as are *"I"* and *"C"*) is the one you *struggle with most* and *understand least*. Although it may be unfamiliar to you, you *can* learn to employ it — and in some cases, you already have! This, by the way, is good news! We can *grow, learn* and *develop* new ways of becoming all we were meant to be!

Provides *ADVENTURE*
Brings *DETERMINATION*
Uses *CREATIVITY*
Stresses *INNOVATION*

Provides *IMAGINATION*
Brings *SPONTANEITY*
Uses *INSPIRATION*
Stresses *INTERACTION*

While arrows connect adjacent traits, there are no arrows connecting "*D*" and "*S*", or "*I*" and "*C*". This is because they are not "naturaly" complementary traits. They are usually thought of as contrasting traits. Although these "opposite" skills may be unfamiliar, they still may be developed.

Provides *ANALYSIS*
Brings *LOGIC*
Uses *OBJECTIVITY*
Stresses *CONSISTENCY*

Provides *STABILITY*
Brings *HARMONY*
Uses *COMPATIBILITY*
Stresses *SECURITY*

In this section, we will learn about "blends" of personality types — how different traits work in your personality to create your own, unique personality style. We'll see how a "*D*" type person can also have some fairly strong "*I*," "*S*," or "*C*" qualities. An "*I*" can have fairly strong "*D*," "*S*," or "*C*" traits. "*S*'s" and "*C*'s" can also share strengths from the other types.

Most commonly, people have one very dominant style, backed up by a secondary style. With such people, two plotting points will be *above the midline* and two plotting points will fall *below the midline*. It is also possible for people to have only one very dominant style above the midline, with the other three styles falling below the midline. And some people have three styles above the midline, with only one below the midline. If those variables seem confusing, imagine that each of those styles vary in strength and intensity from person to person. But that's where our differences in personality come from — that's what makes people so fascinating to study. As you look at the charts on the following pages, you can develop a "lab" in your mind — and everywhere you go, you will be able to see people through your "personality microscope!"

Classic "*D*" Type Blends

The "***D***" is above the mid-line, and the "***I***," "***S***," and "***C***" are below. ⟶

(The graphs below show different **blends**, where "***I***," "***S***," or "***C***" may also be above the mid-line, but not as strong as the "***D***." As the arrows indicate, the traits may vary in strength and intensity.)

The "*D*" Type

"*D*" with "*I*"

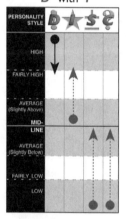

"*D*" with "*S*"

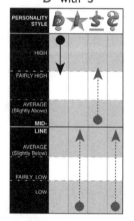

"*D*" with "*C*"

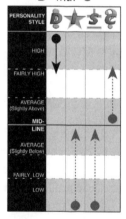

"*D*" with "*I*" and "*S*"

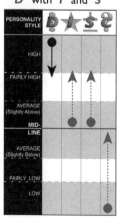

"*D*" with "*I*" and "*C*"

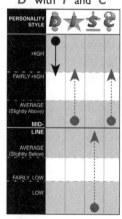

"*D*" with "*S*" and "*C*"

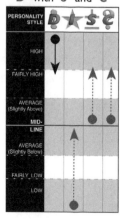

Identifying Your "D" Characteristics

Self-image is a funny thing… It tends to minimize excellence and magnify flaws. As a result, it is sometimes difficult for us to see our positive traits and potential.

Each of the personality styles is gifted differently. Each style has the inborn ability to make significant contributions in life. Unfortunately, we do not always demonstrate our best traits. However, when we focus on being our "best self," the highest qualities of our own personality style enable us to become important, key players in the game of life.

Knowing this should help us understand and accept ourselves while developing a better appreciation for the contributions of those around us. If you have a "**D**" type personality style — or if you know someone who is a "**D**" — here is what to look for:

The "**D**" Type Is Good At…

- Overcoming obstacles

- Seeing the big picture

- Pushing the group ahead

- Accepting challenges without fear

- Maintaining focus on goals

- Getting results

- Providing leadership

- Handling several jobs at the same time

Classic "*I*" Type Blends

The "*I*" is above the mid-line, and the "*D*," "*S*," and "*C*" are below. →

(The graphs below show different **blends**, where "*D*," "*S*," or "*C*" may also be above the mid-line, but not as strong as the "*I*." As the arrows indicate, the traits may vary in strength and intensity.)

The "*I*" Type

"*I*" with "*D*"

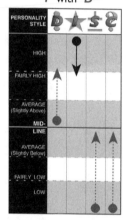

"*I*" with "*S*"

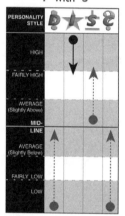

"*I*" with "*C*"

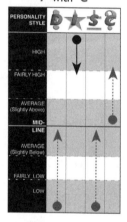

"*I*" with "*D*" and "*S*"

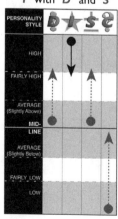

"*I*" with "*D*" and "*C*"

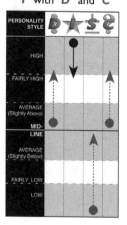

"*I*" with "*S*" and "*C*"

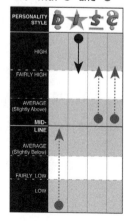

Identifying Your "I" Characteristics

Self-image is a funny thing… It tends to minimize excellence and magnify flaws. As a result, it is sometimes difficult for us to see our positive traits and potential.

Each of the personality styles is gifted differently. Each style has the inborn ability to make significant contributions in life. Unfortunately, we do not always demonstrate our best traits. However, when we focus on being our "best self," the highest qualities of our own personality style enable us to become important, key players in the game of life.

Knowing this should help us understand and accept ourselves while developing a better appreciation for the contributions of those around us. If you have an "*I*" type personality style — or if you know someone who is an "*I*" — here is what to look for:

The "*I*" Type Is Good At…

- Speaking persuasively

- Responding well to surprises

- Expressing ideas

- Accepting new people

- Creating enthusiasm

- Working well with others

- Having a sense of humor

- Keeping a positive attitude

Classic "S" Type Blends

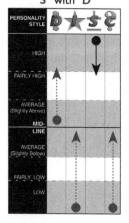

The "S" is above the mid-line, and the "D," "I," and "C" are below. →

(The graphs below show different **blends,** where "D," "I," or "C" may also be above the mid-line, but not as strong as the "S." As the arrows indicate, the traits may vary in strength and intensity.)

The "S" Type

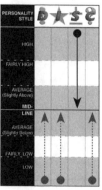

"S" with "D"

"S" with "I"
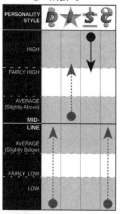

"S" with "C"
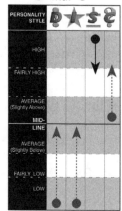

"S" with "D" and "I"
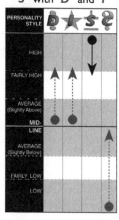

"S" with "D" and "C"
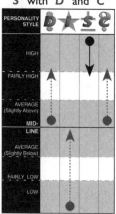

"S" with "I" and "C"
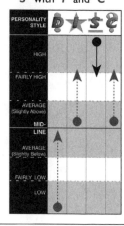

Identifying Your "S" Characteristics

Self-image is a funny thing… It tends to minimize excellence and magnify flaws. As a result, it is sometimes difficult for us to see our positive traits and potential.

Each of the personality styles is gifted differently. Each style has the inborn ability to make significant contributions in life. Unfortunately, we do not always demonstrate our best traits. However, when we focus on being our "best self," the highest qualities of our own personality style enable us to become important, key players in the game of life.

Knowing this should help us understand and accept ourselves while developing a better appreciation for the contributions of those around us. If you have an "S" type personality style — or if you know someone who is an "S" — here is what to look for:

The "S" Type Is Good At…

- Showing sincerity

- Being even-tempered

- Emphasizing loyalty

- Building relationships

- Seeing an easier way to do things

- Providing dependability

- Being a team player

- Making others feel accepted

Classic "C" Type Blends

The "C" is above the mid-line, and the "D," "I," and "S" are below. →

(The graphs below show different **blends**, where "D," "I" or "S" may also be above the mid-line, but not as strong as the "C." As the arrows indicate, the traits may vary in strength and intensity.)

The "C" Type

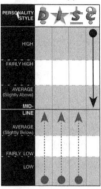

"C" with "D"
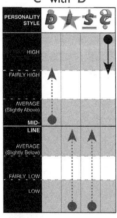

"C" with "I"
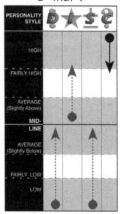

"C" with "S"
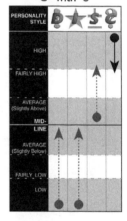

"C" with "D" and "I"
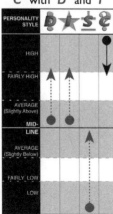

"C" with "D" and "S"
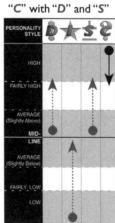

"C" with "I" and "S"
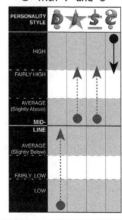

Identifying Your "*C*" Characteristics

Self-image is a funny thing… It tends to minimize excellence and magnify flaws. As a result, it is sometimes difficult for us to see our positive traits and potential.

Each of the personality styles is gifted differently. Each style has the inborn ability to make significant contributions in life. Unfortunately, we do not always demonstrate our best traits. However, when we focus on being our "best self," the highest qualities of our own personality style enable us to become important, key players in the game of life.

Knowing this should help us understand and accept ourselves while developing a better appreciation for the contributions of those around us. If you have a "*C*" type personality style — or if you know someone who is a "*C*" — here is what to look for:

The "*C*" Type Is Good At…

• Working systematically

• Being conscientious

• Maintaining their focus

• Analyzing obstacles

• Striving for logical results

• Organizing material

• Thinking logically

• Evaluating situations

Trying On Behaviors...

Does your personality change over the years? The answer is both *yes* and *no*. Over the years we should mature and grow wiser in decision making abilities. However, simply because your behavior is different from youth to maturity, it does not necessarily mean your personality has changed.

For example, if an 18-year-old, strong-willed, high "**D**" teenager joins the Marine Corps, will his personality change? He will get himself under control during this time, maturing, adapting and adjusting to his environment, obeying orders and cooperating without questioning authority. However, his strong nature will still be present when he leaves the Marine Corps and gets back into the "real world." His behavior will return to its natural style — with the *addition* of maturity and discipline through experience.

So... *yes*, personality "changes" when it matures, adjusts and adapts. And... *no*, we do not become another person with a different outlook or understanding about life and how we respond.

Teenagers "try on" different types of behavior as they grow up. Have you heard of the "Terrible Twos," when toddlers push the limits on parents and others, trying to learn where the boundaries are? In adolescence, many mental, physical, emotional and spiritual changes occur. During this time, teens "try on" different behaviors to see how they feel, imitating people they admire. Usually, when an experimental behavior does not work well, or is frustrating and futile, they give up with little damage done. Any adult can look back on their teenage years and remember how they settled down to the "natural" style they had when they were younger. That's why the Bible says "Train up a child in the way he should go, and when he is older, he will not depart from it."

The basic personality we are born with is probably seen best between the ages of 4–14, then goes into a tailspin from 14–18, and then smooths out and produces a great life from 18 and older. Although they are not "required," the turbulent teen years seem to be a "fact of life" that most people experience.

Answer
Key

Funbook Answer Keys...

These are answers for the "fill-in-the-blank" lines in the Funbook. They are provided for readers who have not attended a Seminar in person, where the information is provided firsthand.

PAGE 9:   **THE NUMERICAL SERIES**

The puzzle on page 9 is solved easily when you know the pattern. Divide the box into four sections, drawing a line down the center from top to bottom, and across the middle from left to right. Small tick-marks at the midpoints on each side will help you, although most people do not notice them. The number "1" will be found in the upper left box. "2" will be found in the upper right box. Go to the lower left box to find "3." Then go to the lower right box to find "4." Following that pattern, "5" is in the upper left, "6" is in the upper right, "7" is in the lower left, and "8" is in the lower right, etc. Now that you know the pattern, time yourself for one minute. This time, put an "X" on the number 1... then an "X" on 2... then an "X" on 3, etc. See how many numbers you can find in series in 60 seconds. Ready...? Go!

A simple thing can be difficult to figure out if the pattern is not recognized. *Life is like that, too!* There are reasons and patterns for our behavior, and when we understand them, the puzzle of life is much easier to solve. When we know there are clues to look for, we can find them more easily.

PAGE 10:   **DESCRIPTIVE TERMS**

This is a breakdown for most of the general population's basic behaviors or tendencies. Divided into two classifications, we have people who are active and outgoing, and people who are more passive and reserved. To complete the first section on this page, enter the following information in the appropriate spaces:

Active/Outgoing	**Passive/Reserved**
• Fast-paced	• Slower-paced
• Optimistic	• Cautious
• Energetic	• Concerned
• Involved	• Reluctant
• Positive	• Critical
• Enthusiastic	• Discerning

The second set of classifiers are: people who are task-oriented and "high-tech," and those who are more people-oriented and "high-touch." Complete this section by entering this information:

Task/High-Tech	People/High-Touch
• Form	• Relationships
• Function	• Caring
• Programs	• Sharing
• Plans	• Emotions
• Projects	• Feelings
• Process	• Friendships

Together, these four classifications help us to determine each person's unique temperament or personality style. **D**'s have more outgoing and task-oriented traits; **I**'s are also outgoing, but are people-oriented; **S**'s are also people-oriented, but they are reserved; **C**'s are reserved, but are also task-oriented.

"Alliteration" is the repetition of a sound in a phrase or poem — as in "Peter Piper picked a peck of pickled peppers." (See, this *is* an educational project!) On pages 12, 15, 18 and 21, you can list alliterative words that describe major personality style traits. Using these will help you identify and remember the fundamental qualities of each style. You can also fill in the identifying symbol, the percentage of the population that has this as their primary style, well-known examples of this personality style, and two words that describe this personality's basic needs or motivators. Fill in these pages as follows:

Page 12:   **Descriptive "D" Words**

• Dominant	• Demanding
• Direct	• Determined
• Decisive	• Doer
• Dictatorial	• Dogmatic
• Dreamer	• Diligent
• Dynamic	• Defiant

DEFINING SYMBOL: Exclamation Point

Percentage of Population: *10%*

Examples: Tom Cruise, "Mrs. Olsen" from "Little House on the Prairie," Hillary Clinton, and the Apostle Paul

Basic Need: Challenge/Control

Page 15:   **Descriptive "*I*" Words**

- Inspirational
- Inducing
- Interesting
- Important
- Interested in people
- Imaginative
- Influencing
- Impressive
- Impressionable
- Interchangeable
- Impulsive
- Illogical

DEFINING SYMBOL: Star

Percentage of Population: 25–30%

Examples: Tim Allen, "Lucy Ricardo" from "I Love Lucy," Sally Field, and the Apostle Peter

Basic Need: Recognition/Approval

Page 18:   **Descriptive "*S*" Words**

- Steady
- Secure
- Servant
- Submissive
- Status Quo
- Sameness
- Stable
- Supportive
- Sweet
- Shy
- Sentimental
- Sucker

DEFINING SYMBOL: Plus/Minus Sign

Percentage of Population: 30–35%

Examples: Dr. Martin Luther King, Jr., "Aunt Bee" from "The Andy Griffith Show," Mary Tyler Moore, and the Apostle John

Basic Need: Appreciation/Security

Page 21:   **Descriptive "*C*" Words**

- Competent
- Cautious
- Calculating
- Compliance-Seeking
- Correct
- Consistent
- Cognitive
- Careful
- Critical Thinking
- Conscientious
- Conformist
- Cold

DEFINING SYMBOL: Question Mark

Percentage of Population: 20–25%

Examples: Jacqueline Kennedy Onassis, "Mr. Spock" from "Star Trek," Ralph Nader, and the Apostle Thomas

Basic Need: Quality Answers/Value

Of course, according to your own blended style, some descriptive terms from your primary trait will not seem to fit you, while some terms from your secondary trait(s) may fit you well.

Getting Personal

L👁️👁️KING at ME...

Each personality style has behavioral traits that include strengths and weaknesses. As you look over the list of traits on these two pages, put a check mark ✓ in front of each word that you →

____ Arrogant
____ Abrasive
____ Ambitious
____ Angry
____ Competitive
____ Conceited
____ Confident
____ Courageous
____ Crafty
____ Cruel
____ Decisive
____ Deliberate
____ Demanding
____ Determined

____ Dictatorial
____ Direct
____ Domineering
____ Driving
____ Goal Oriented
____ Impatient
____ Inconsiderate
____ Independent
____ Leader
____ Logical
____ Offensive
____ Optimistic
____ Persistent
____ Pioneering
____ Practical
____ Productive

____ Proud
____ Pushy
____ Reckless
____ Responsible
____ Responsive
____ Results Oriented
____ Rude
____ Sarcastic
____ Self-Confident
____ Self-Reliant
____ Self-Sufficient
____ Skeptical
____ Straightforward
____ Strong willed
____ Stubborn
____ Unemotional

____ Carefree
____ Communicative
____ Compassionate
____ Daydreamer
____ Directionless
____ Egocentric
____ Emotional
____ Enthusiastic
____ Exaggerated
____ Excitable
____ Fearful
____ Fervent
____ Friendly
____ Fun

____ Gossipy
____ Happy
____ Imaginative
____ Impulsive
____ Independent
____ Involved
____ Lacking purpose
____ Loud
____ Manipulative
____ Mobile
____ Optimistic
____ Outgoing
____ Personable
____ Persuasive
____ Poised
____ Polished

____ Popular
____ Restless
____ Sarcastic
____ Self-centered
____ Sociable
____ Spontaneous
____ Talkative
____ Trusting
____ Undependable
____ Undisciplined
____ Unfocused
____ Unrealistic
____ Unstable
____ Verbal
____ Warm
____ Weak willed

This entire section is about focusing on your personality style... What this information means to you personally, and what you can do with it... "Why you do those things!" We want the next several pages to be very helpful to you!

honestly feel describes you. Feel free to check as many or as few as you wish in all four categories. It will be interesting to see how you match your profile!

___ Amiable	___Gullible	___Self-protective
___Calm	___Humorous	___Shy
___Cooperative	___Indecisive	___Single-minded
___Dependable	___Inflexible	___Slow
___Dependent	___Lacking initiative	___Softhearted
___Conservative	___Loyal	___Spectator
___Consistent	___Passive	___Stable
___Deliberate	___Patient	___Steadfast
___Diplomatic	___Possessive	___Steady
___Easily manipulated	___Practical	___Stingy
___Easygoing	___Predictable	___Systematic
___Efficient	___Relaxed	___ Tactful
___Fearful	___Reliable	___ Timid
___Good listener	___Resentful	___ Trustworthy
	___Resistant to change	___Uncommunicative
	___Selfish	___Unmotivated

___ Accurate	___Fretful	___Precise
___ Aesthetic	___Gifted	___Questioning
___ Analytical	___Idealistic	___Rigid
___Calculating	___Impractical	___Self-centered
___Cautious	___Inflexible	___Self-sacrificing
___Conscientious	___Intense	___Sensitive
___Conservative	___Logical	___Stable
___Correct	___Low-keyed	___Systematic
___Critical	___Loyal	___ Teachable
___Curious	___Moody	___ Theoretical
___Dependable	___Negative	___ Thorough
___Doubtful	___Neat	___ Traditional
___Easily offended	___Nosy	___ Truthful
___Fearful	___Orderly	___Unsociable
	___Perfectionist	___ Vengeful
	___Picky	___ Worrisome

GOAL SETTING

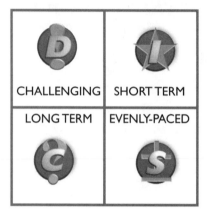

CHALLENGING	SHORT TERM
LONG TERM	EVENLY-PACED

Each personality style has a different approach to setting goals. For a "**D**," it is the meeting of a challenge that is important. For an "**I**," the goal should be reached in smaller steps with immediate rewards. The "**S**" believes that "slow and steady wins the race." The "**C**" can appreciate future distant rewards.

TASK METHOD

Each personality has a preferred approach to doing a job. "**D**'s" have confidence in "conquering" a task. "**I**'s" look at it as a game to win and make it enjoyable rather than boring. "**S**'s" want the least stressful way to do a project, and may sacrifice to avoid conflict. "**C**'s" plan their work and work their plan.

MY WAY	FUN WAY
RIGHT WAY	EASY WAY

ATTITUDES & PREFERENCES

The likes and dislikes of each personality type are very different:

- I like to think about the future.
- I like new ideas.
- I like a challenge.
- I like activities that change a lot.
- I like projects that produce results.
- I like to be my own boss.
- I like things to move fast.
- I don't like to be under anyone else's control.
- I don't like to get bogged down in details.
- I like to be evaluated on my results.

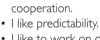

- I like practical ways to do things.
- I don't like conflicts with people.
- I like to express my ideas and feelings.
- I like being part of a group.
- I don't like details.
- I dislike a lot of control or pushy people.
- I like people to agree and get along.
- I enjoy peace and harmony.
- I like a lot of social activity and fun.
- I like surprises.

- I like practical ideas and suggestions
- I like to know exactly what is expected of me.
- I don't like a lot of clutter.
- I like to finish whatever I start.
- I like an established routine.
- I don't like conflicts.
- I like technical things that require thought and planning.
- I think I worry a lot.
- I like specialized tasks.
- I like clear instructions.

- I like teamwork and cooperation.
- I like predictability.
- I like to work on one task at a time.
- I like sticking with what I know will work.
- I don't like arguments.
- I like things to stay the same.
- I love practicality — the more practical, the better.
- I don't like conflict.
- I don't like sudden changes.
- I like knowing what is going to happen in advance.

MOTIVATIONAL TIPS

Each personality style has different "hot bottons" They may say:

- I like to be in charge.
- I like situations that change a lot.
- When I work, I work hard.
- When I play, I play hard.
- I like to have power.
- I am not afraid to take a reasonable risk.
- I like to make decisions.
- I don't like the same routine.
- I don't like doing slow or repetitive tasks.
- I like new challenges.
- I like to solve problems.
- I like to be in authority.

- I like a lot of friends.
- I like acceptance.
- I like other people to handle the details.
- I like a friendly environment.
- I like encouragement.
- I prefer short projects to long ones.
- It is important to me to be popular.
- I don't like a lot of rules.
- I like to "go" and "do."
- I dislike too many regulations.
- I like public recognition.
- I am easily distracted.

- I like quality.
- I don't like a lot of silliness.
- I like detailed tasks.
- I like logical information.
- I like charts and graphs.
- I like to find creative solutions.
- I like to be reassured.
- I like to be organized.
- I have high standards for myself and others.
- I tend to be a perfectionist.
- I like to be commended for doing good work.
- I like to know and do things step-by-step.

- I like a stable lifestyle.
- I like to please others.
- I enjoy people enjoying life.
- I don't like starting new projects.
- It makes me happy to see others happy.
- I don't work well with aggressive people.
- I like to feel appreciated.
- I like routine procedures.
- I don't like "daring" events.
- I like to feel secure.
- I enjoy finishing a task.
- I don't mind being told what to do.

COMMUNICATIONS TIPS

When talking to each of the personality types, it is the best to:

- Get to the main point.
- Be brief and specific.
- Think in terms of answering the "WHAT?" question.
- Focus on action-based results.
- Solve problems.
- Be logical.
- Agree with objective facts - not subjective people.
- Look for obstacles to overcome.
- Support your statements credibly.

- Keep a friendly environment.
- Let them express their ideas.
- Think in terms of answering the "WHO?" question.
- Help them turn their talk into action.
- Tell them what others have done.
- Allow time for socializing.
- Have short term projects with incentives.
- Indicate mutual friendship.
- Focus on their accomplishments.

- Create a "Pro/Con" balance sheet for suggested actions.
- Be specific on points of agreement.
- Think in terms of answering the "WHY?" question.
- Supply clear, accurate data.
- Eliminate surprises.
- Show how they fit in.
- Anticipate their questions and have credible answers.
- Be patient and speak slowly while providing details.

- Review your thoughts clearly.

- Be agreeable and non-threatening.
- Show sincere interest.
- Think in terms of answering the "HOW?" question.
- Demonstrate patience.
- Be clear and explain details calmly.
- Give them time to adjust to changes.
- Explain their contribution and valued service in the plan.
- Provide follow-up and transitional support.
- Show the benefits of their actions.

LEARNING STYLES

Each personality style approaches instruction differently:

"I want to do things my way!"

"What is this material all about?"

"Let me help teach the class."

"Be quick and to the point."

"Let me be in charge."

"I want to do things the fun way!"

"I learn best in a relaxed atmosphere."

"Let's learn by playing games."

"I enjoy being creative."

"I'll understand if I can see it."

"I want to do things the right way!"

"Answer my questions with quality information."

"Give me facts and figures."

"Let me do extra credit work."

"Explain your expectations."

"I want to do things the easy way!"

"Slow down a little bit so I can process these changes."

"Go over it one more time."

"Help me understand this."

"I want to please you."

IDEAL ENVIRONMENT

Each style has a "comfort zone": "I like an environment where..."

- I can be in charge of myself and others.
- There are a lot of different activities and challenges.
- I have freedom to set my own priorities and pace.
- I can see that I am growing.
- The bottom line is important.
- I have opportunities for advancement.
- I can look good.

- There are people to talk to.
- Good work is recognized and praised.
- There is opportunity to influence others.
- Everyone has a good attitude.
- People are accepted.
- There are positive working conditions.
- I am free from a lot of details and repetitive tasks.

- There is a specific plan.
- I don't have someone working over my shoulder.
- There is no "hurried" activity.
- There are exact roles and job descriptions.
- Expectations are clear.
- Changes are made slowly and carefully.
- I can be rewarded for new ideas and improvements.

- I can identify with a group.
- Sincere appreciation is shown.
- There is a regular routine of events.
- I don't feel rushed and under pressure.
- There is not much change.
- We specialize in a few things.
- I know what and where my boundaries are.

Secret Tip:
Before you can be IN authority you must first learn to be UNDER authority.

Secret Tip:
It's NICE to be important, but it's more IMPORTANT to be nice.

Secret Tip:
Don't be afraid to say, "What part of NO don't you understand?"

Secret Tip:
People don't CARE how much you know until they KNOW how much you care.

Getting
Focused

Your final assignment is to focus this information on your real life. While it is only a two-page exercise is this book, you'll find it is an ongoing, lifetime challenge! Regardless of what career decisions you make, research studies report that only 15% of your success will rely on your technical skills and abilities — typically, 85% of work success is due to your skills with people, and how well you understand yourself and others. We are hopeful that this book will be an ongoing, lifetime resource for you to meet these challenges.

If you have found this material helpful, you may be interested in reading some of Dr. Rohm's other books, including *Positive Personality Profiles, Who Do You Think You Are Anyway?*, and *Different Children, Different Needs* (co-authored with Charles F. Boyd). Dr. Rohm's helpful video and cassette tape series include "How to Understand Yourself and Others" and "Breaking Through The Walls That Hinder Communication." You may request a catalog or contact Dr. Rohm through PERSONALITY INSIGHTS Post Office Box 28592 Atlanta, GA 30358-0592.

www.personalityinsights.com

Personal Interests Inventory and Goals

Name_____ Age_____ Grade_____

Please complete the following information to the best of your ability:

1. Which D-I-S-C score was the highest on your plotting graph?

   Graph I:_____   Graph II:_____

2. Circle the one personality area that (at this point) feels the most comfort-

   able to you.

   (circle one:)   **D**   **I**   **S**   **C**

3. According to the area you just circled, turn to the list of **professions**

   that are best suited to that particular personality style. ("**D**" turn to page

   13, "**I**" to page 16, "**S**" to page 19, and "**C**" to page 22.) Read through the

   appropriate list.

4. From the personality style you circled in Question 2 (above), write down

   in the following spaces **three professions** which you like best:

   1.) _____

   2.) _____

   3.) _____

5. Write down **one profession** that interests you from each of the **other**

   personality styles:

   Personality Type _____ Profession _____

   Personality Type _____ Profession _____

   Personality Type _____ Profession _____

6. Complete this statement: "If I could try to do anything in life and I knew I

   would not fail, I would want to become a:_____

   _____."

7. Who do you know who is right now doing what you want to do?

_____

_____

_____

8. What steps did he/she/they take to get where they are today?

_____

_____

_____

9. You will be the same person ten years from now except for two things: the people you meet and the books you read. Name one person you would like to meet and one book you want to read:

(Person) _____

(Book) _____

10. List three goals you want to accomplish by the time you are 25 years old.

1.) _____

2.) _____

3.) _____

_____

In 1952, the graduating class of ivy league Yale University was asked if they had a list of written goals for their lives. Only 3% said yes. Twenty years later, researchers discovered this same 3% had a greater net worth than the combined wealth of the other 97% of students who had graduated with them!

What made the difference? It was not their ranking in the class, or the courses they studied, or their intelligence, or their family background. There were two major differences: 1) they had written down goals they wanted to reach, and 2) they had found a mentor — someone who was doing those things they wanted to do — and they had followed in that person's steps.